Influential Presidents
Thomas Jefferson

by Martha London

FOCUS READERS

BEACON

www.focusreaders.com

Focus Readers is distributed by North Star Editions: sales@northstareditions.com | 888-417-0195

Produced for Focus Readers by Red Line Editorial.

Photographs ©: Rembrandt Peale/Library of Congress, cover, 1; iStockphoto, 4, 11, 29; William Russell Birch/Library of Congress, 7; Michael Snell/Alamy, 8; Shutterstock Images, 13, 19, 20–21, 22, 25, 26; North Wind Picture Archives/Alamy, 14, 17

Library of Congress Cataloging-in-Publication Data
Names: London, Martha, author.
Title: Thomas Jefferson / Martha London.
Description: Lake Elmo : Focus Readers, [2023] | Series: Influential
   presidents | Includes bibliographical references and index. | Audience:
   Grades 2-3
Identifiers: LCCN 2022025525 (print) | LCCN 2022025526 (ebook) | ISBN
   9781637394632 (hardcover) | ISBN 9781637395004 (paperback) | ISBN
   9781637395714 (pdf) | ISBN 9781637395370 (ebook)
Subjects: LCSH: Jefferson, Thomas, 1743-1826--Juvenile literature. |
   Presidents--United States--Biography--Juvenile literature.
Classification: LCC E332.79 .L66 2023 (print) | LCC E332.79 (ebook) | DDC
   973.4/6092 [B]--dc23/eng/20220601
LC record available at https://lccn.loc.gov/2022025525
LC ebook record available at https://lccn.loc.gov/2022025526

Printed in the United States of America
Mankato, MN
012023

About the Author

Martha London is a writer and educator. She lives in Minnesota with her cat.

Table of Contents

Chapter 1

Major Changes

The United States faced a big choice in 1800. Thomas Jefferson was running for president against John Adams. Jefferson said he would make major changes if he won.

 In 1800, Jefferson was facing Adams for the second time. Jefferson had lost in 1796.

John Adams was the current president. He had worked to create a strong national government. But Jefferson had different ideas. He believed state governments should have more power.

The vote was close. In the end, Jefferson won. He became the

Did You Know?

Jefferson was more popular in the South. Adams was more popular in the North.

 The US Capitol was still being built when Jefferson became president.

new president in March 1801.
The election had caused many
arguments. But Jefferson called for
unity. It was the beginning of a new
era in US history.

Chapter 2

Independence

Thomas Jefferson was born on April 13, 1743. He grew up in Virginia on a large farm. Virginia was a British **colony** at the time.

Thomas's father held people of African descent in slavery.

Thomas Jefferson spent part of his childhood at Tuckahoe Plantation in Virginia.

When Thomas grew up, he took control of many of these slaves.

Jefferson became a lawmaker in Virginia. During this time, the British collected **taxes** from Americans. But Americans had no voice in the British government.

Jefferson believed this was wrong. He wrote about Americans' rights. He believed the people in America should be in charge of themselves. Many Americans started to agree with him.

 The war between the colonies and Great Britain became known as the Revolutionary War.

In 1775, the colonies went to war with Great Britain. A year later, Jefferson met with American leaders. They asked him to write the Declaration of **Independence**.

It said Great Britain was no longer in control of America.

In 1783, the Americans won the war. A few years later, George Washington became the first US president. Jefferson worked for him. He helped Washington deal with other countries.

Did You Know?

American leaders finished the Declaration of Independence on July 2, 1776. But they did not sign it until July 4.

 John Adams served as president from 1797 to 1801.

John Adams was the president after Washington. Jefferson served as Adams's vice president. But he disagreed with many of Adams's ideas. Jefferson knew he wanted to be president someday.

Chapter 3

The Louisiana Purchase

In 1801, Thomas Jefferson finally became president. He wanted the United States to grow. At the time, France controlled a huge part of North America. The United States bought this land in 1803.

 The United States paid $15 million for the Louisiana Territory.

The deal became known as the Louisiana Purchase. Jefferson wanted to learn about the land. He hoped white settlers could move there someday.

However, the land was not empty. Many American Indians lived there. This land had been their home for thousands of years. Even so, Jefferson believed the land should belong to the United States.

Jefferson did not want to have wars with Native peoples. But he

 Millions of Native people died of diseases brought by white settlers.

thought conflicts were likely to happen. Jefferson believed he had a solution. He wanted American Indians to be more like white people. If that happened, Jefferson thought Native peoples and white settlers would be less likely to fight.

Jefferson wanted Native peoples to farm large areas of land. He also wanted them to be Christian. In these ways, Jefferson hoped to change Native peoples' way of life.

Jefferson sent explorers to the Louisiana **Territory**. They traveled for three years. The explorers created maps of the territory. They

Did You Know?

The Louisiana Purchase doubled the size of the United States.

 Meriwether Lewis and William Clark led the group that explored the Louisiana Territory.

met people from several different Native Nations. They also studied the territory's plants and animals. The explorers sent reports back to Jefferson.

The Library of Congress

The Library of Congress keeps copies of all books in the United States. The first Library of Congress burned down in 1814. Most of the books were lost.

Jefferson had a large library of his own. He wanted to help the United States. So, he sold many of his own books. These books were the beginning of the new Library of Congress. Many of the books are still there today.

Today, the Library of Congress has millions of books.

21

Chapter 4

A Complicated Legacy

Thomas Jefferson ran for a second **term** in 1804. At the time, the **economy** was doing well. People were paying lower taxes. Many voters agreed with Jefferson's ideas. He won the election easily.

 Jefferson's second term lasted from 1805 to 1809.

Jefferson signed a new law in 1807. This law made it illegal to bring enslaved people into the United States. However, slavery was still allowed in most states.

Jefferson believed slavery was wrong. He wanted it to end. But Jefferson enslaved more than 600 people during his lifetime. He thought white people were smarter than Black people. At the time, most white Americans shared this belief.

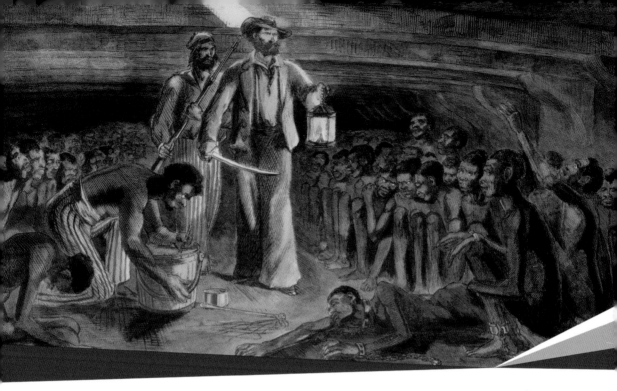

 Slaveholders forced Africans onto ships and brought them to North America.

In the early 1800s, the British and French were at war. Jefferson did not want the United States to join the conflict. So, he signed a law in 1807. The law made it illegal to trade goods with other countries.

The Jefferson Memorial in Washington, DC, honors the third president.

This law helped keep the United States out of the war. But it hurt the economy.

Jefferson **retired** when his second term ended. Today, people

remember him for many reasons.
He helped the United States grow.
He also kept the country out of
wars. But he tried to take away
Native peoples' way of life. And his
beliefs about ending slavery did not
match his actions. Jefferson left
behind a complicated **legacy**.

Jefferson died on July 4, 1826. That
was 50 years after the Declaration of
Independence was signed.

FOCUS ON
Thomas Jefferson

Write your answers on a separate piece of paper.

1. Write a sentence that describes the main ideas from Chapter 3.

2. Jefferson believed state governments should have more power than the national government. Do you agree? Why or why not?

3. Where did Thomas Jefferson grow up?
   - **A.** Virginia
   - **B.** Washington
   - **C.** Louisiana

4. What might have happened if Jefferson had not sold his books to the United States?
   - **A.** Slavery would have ended much sooner.
   - **B.** The Library of Congress would not exist.
   - **C.** The Louisiana Purchase would not have happened.

5. What does **unity** mean in this book?

*The election had caused many arguments. But Jefferson called for **unity**.*

    A. when people have long arguments

    B. when people come together and agree

    C. when people vote to choose a leader

6. What does **conflicts** mean in this book?

*Jefferson did not want to have wars with Native peoples. But he thought **conflicts** were likely to happen.*

    A. fights

    B. agreements

    C. meetings

Answer key on page 32.

Glossary

colony
An area controlled by a country that is far away.

economy
A system of goods, services, money, and jobs.

era
A period of history.

independence
The ability to make decisions without being controlled by another government.

legacy
The things a person becomes known for.

retired
Stopped working.

taxes
Money added to the cost of a purchase and given to the government.

term
The amount of time a person can serve after being elected.

territory
An area of land that is not a state but is still part of the United States.

To Learn More

BOOKS

Elston, Heidi M. D. *Thomas Jefferson.* Minneapolis: Abdo Publishing, 2021.

Forest, Christopher. *Louisiana Purchase.* Minneapolis: Jump!, 2021.

Sirimarco, Elizabeth. *Thomas Jefferson.* Mankato, MN: The Child's World, 2020.

NOTE TO EDUCATORS

Visit **www.focusreaders.com** to find lesson plans, activities, links, and other resources related to this title.

Index

A
Adams, John, 5–6, 13
American Indians,
   16–19, 27

B
Black Americans, 24

D
Declaration of
   Independence,
   11–12, 27

E
election, 7, 23

F
France, 15, 25

G
Great Britain, 10, 12, 25

L
Library of Congress, 20
Louisiana Purchase,
   15–16, 18

N
Native Nations,
   16–19, 27

S
slavery, 9–10, 24, 27

V
vice president, 13
Virginia, 9, 12

W
Washington, George,
   12–13

Answer Key: 1. Answers will vary; **2.** Answers will vary; **3.** A; **4.** B; **5.** B; **6.** A